SO-ASQ-083

STANFORD STREET NAMES

A POCKET GUIDE

by

Richard W. Cottle

Richard W. Cottle

STANFORD HISTORICAL SOCIETY

Stanford, California

STANFORD STREET NAMES

This book made possible through the generous support
of the Stanford University offices of the President,
the Provost, the Dean of Research, the Dean of Engineering,
and the Dean of Earth Sciences, as well as the
volunteer support of the Stanford Historical Society

STANFORD HISTORICAL SOCIETY
P.O. Box 20028
Stanford, California 94309
(650) 725-3332
http://histsoc.stanford.edu

Editor: Roxanne Nilan
Designer: Joanna McClean

Copyright © 2005 by Richard W. Cottle
10 9 8 7 6 5 4 3 2 1
Printed in the United States of America
ISBN: 0-9664249-3-X

*Requested by Mr. Stanford to give names
to the streets already finished, I decided with
his approval, to commemorate thus modestly
several fine figures in the early history of California.*

David Starr Jordan
The Days of a Man (1922)

*The President named this, our street, which had not
a tree or shrub or blade of green, or any
sidewalk or road except the wheel-broken track
in the blistered adobe—he named it "Alvarado
Avenue"! I nearly fainted. "But it is so obviously
a row!" I exclaimed. "It will be an avenue some
day," Dr. Jordan said, but twinkling. He changed
the name to Alvarado Row.*

Ellen Coit Elliott
It Happened This Way (1940)

First faculty houses along Alvarado Row, 1891, with Quad in distance.

INTRODUCTION

T his booklet is the outgrowth of a simple question I asked myself in the early 1990s: Why does Stanford University have a street named "Panama"? I found no answer to this, or to other questions that followed in rapid succession: Who were Palou, Crespi, and Ortega? To what do Escondido, Gerona, and Mirada refer? How did other Stanford streets get their names?

It began to dawn on me that others might be equally lacking in knowledge of how streets got their names. An informal survey quickly confirmed this suspicion. No comprehensive publication contained the information. *Streets of Palo Alto*, a booklet published by the Palo Alto Historical Association in 1979 (revised in 1991), said nothing about the streets of Stanford. *Stanford Street Names: A Pocket Guide* is my response to these questions.

Governor's Avenue, seen here around 1890, was also named for the "gum trees" (eucalyptus) that lined it.

Stanford seems never to have had a formal structure for the naming of streets. Without a "paper trail" as a guide, one needs to turn to other sources: autobiographies, local histories, old maps, and files in the Stanford Archives. Though it is certainly true that Stanford has a handful of uninspired street names—old Lanes A, B, C, L, and W, for example, or the new North Service Road—most evoke important aspects of the university's history. As my research progressed, I developed increasing respect for those who selected the names.

The evolution of Leland Stanford's sprawling rural estate and stock farm into a bustling university and residential community is reflected in the naming of streets. Names fall into several categories: Spanish explorers; California's Spanish missions and missionaries; Stanford founders, faculty, and staff; historically important towns and their residents; locally important trees and land formations. After the initial bit of street naming by the university's first president, David Starr Jordan—a romantic in love with his new home—the naming process seems to have been somewhat casual yet generally mindful of the criterion of appropriateness.

Stanford's base map has changed repeatedly since construction of the Quadrangle, responding to the university's continual growth, the complications of traffic flow, and the need for parking. Many Stanford streets have come and gone, or have been redirected. Accordingly, the entries in this booklet are of two kinds. Most of the names are present today on the campus proper (including the residential areas and the Stanford West apartment complex, but not those of the Stanford industrial park area, Stanford Shopping Center, or remote foothill locations). A second category includes names and locations, when available, of Stanford streets that no longer exist or are no longer in use. No doubt some other former streets and street names are missing; I hope that readers with such knowledge will come forth.

Assembling the information for this book greatly broadened my knowledge of this area's geography and its history. The learning process continues to be a stimulating experience. I hope these pages convey my enthusiasm.

ACKNOWLEDGEMENTS

Many people made this project possible. My warm thanks to all of them. In particular, University Archivist Maggie Kimball's ongoing interest has been of enormous help. So has the entire staff of the Department of Special Collections and University Archives, most especially Barry Hinman. Karen Bartholomew, 25-year veteran of Stanford's News Service and chair of the Stanford Historical Society's publication committee, played a continuously supportive role. She shared notes on the subject compiled by Historical Society members: David Weber's initial work on Stanford streets, and another—on place names including streets—begun by Richard and Susan Blois and expanded by Joe and Kathy Cusick. I am grateful to the society for permission to use this material and for everyone's encouragement of this amateur offering in Stanford toponymy.

University archaeologist Laura Jones kindly set me straight on a number of points. Ray Purpur, assistant director of athletics, furnished some useful information on matters in his domain. Both Ed Scoles (formerly of the Faculty/Staff Housing Office, now deceased) and Kathy Sharp (formerly of the Stanford Campus Residential

Leaseholders), provided a clearer notion of the residential subdivisions on campus.

I spent considerable time studying old maps of the university and its environs. Julie Sweetkind at the Branner Earth Sciences Library and Kristina Seyer Smith and Cindy Kirby at the Maps and Records Office provided able assistance, and Heidi Heilemann at Lane Medical Library provided archival material. The friendly staffs at Green Library, Crown Law Library, and Cubberley Education Library were also invaluable. At the Palo Alto Public Library's main branch, Steve Staiger, who is the Palo Alto Historical Association archivist, directed me to useful insurance maps and news clippings. Dorcas Hendershott, Landon Phan, and especially Christy Smith provided scans of archival photographs.

Entirely different help came from Stanford faculty, staff, and students. On nuances of Spanish definitions and orthography, I am indebted to Angel-Victor de Miguel Campos and Angel-Victor de Miguel Rodriquez. Serge Plotkin, Kien Ming Ng, Richard Stone, Tim Keely, and Ashish Goel helped greatly with computer concerns. Helpful suggestions also came from John Brauman, Laura Breyfogle, Bliss Carnochan, Stewart Gillmor, Nancy Lund, Paul Switzer, and Paul Turner.

Most of all, I owe boundless thanks to historian and former university archivist Roxanne Nilan, whose expertise greatly improved the quality of this text.

I wish to extend sincere gratitude to Charles H. Kruger, former dean of research; James D. Plummer, dean of engineering; Franklin M. Orr, Jr., former dean of earth sciences; John W. Etchemendy, provost; and John L. Hennessy, university president, for grants that made this publication possible.

Several people read preliminary drafts of this booklet's text and made friendly suggestions for its correction and improvement. I warmly thank all those who assisted me in bringing forth this guide, but take full responsibility for any errors, bumps, and potholes.

R.W.C.

Old Post Office on busy Lasuen Street, around 1940, is now site of White Plaza (Old Union Courtyard portal in distance).

As used below, the symbol † *indicates that an appella-
tion such as "Street" or "Avenue" is unknown. Some
names appear on old maps without a designation. The
symbol* ★ *signifies a road now lost to history.*

ABBOTT WAY, see **NATHAN ABBOTT WAY**

ABRAMS COURT, in Escondido Village, is named for
LeRoy Abrams (1874–1956), professor of botany and
director of the Dudley Herbarium. He earned A.B. and
M.A. degrees at Stanford in 1899 and 1902, respectively,
and his Ph.D. at Columbia University in 1910. Abrams
taught at Stanford from 1900 to 1904 and from 1906 until
he retired in 1940. He is noted for his four-volume work,
The Illustrated Flora of the Pacific States, the last
volume of which was completed posthumously by his
colleagues.

★ **AIBONITO** † (or **AI BONITO**) is the name used
around 1908 for the upper part of today's Santa Ynez
Street. The name is believed to correspond to the
Spanish exclamation *ai bonito*, meaning "how beautiful." Ellen Coit Elliott, the wife of Stanford's first registrar, recounts that while President David Starr Jordan
was away, "somebody" named the street Aibonito,

LeRoy Abrams

but Jordan changed the "made-up term" when he got back. According to Jordan's autobiography, he found this name inelegant and renamed the road.

★ **ALAMOSA STREET** was located about where the portion of Campus Drive East between Serra and Bowdoin streets is found. Alamosa is Spanish for "cottonwood."

ALLARDICE WAY, in the Frenchman's Hill residential subdivision, honors pioneer faculty member Robert Edgar Allardice (1862–1928). A native of Scotland and graduate of the University of Edinburgh (M.A., 1883), Allardice joined the Stanford faculty in 1892 as a professor of mathematics and taught until his retirement, in 1927. His research dealt mainly with topics in geometry, but he also studied number theory and the theory of equations.

ALTA ROAD is reached from Links Road, south of Junipero Serra Boulevard. On this winding hillside road up to today's Center for Advanced Study in the Behavioral Sciences, Charles G. Lathrop, university business manager and brother of Jane Stanford, built a large house he called *Alta Vista*—Spanish for "high view." The gatehouse still stands, visible from Junipero Serra Boulevard.

Robert Edgar Allardice

★ **ALTURAS DRIVE** was a short road connecting the western end of Gerona Road to what is now Campus Drive East (formerly Mayfield Avenue). Today, Alturas Drive is just a short section of Gerona Road that gives access to the beautiful cul-de-sac, El Escarpado. The name Alturas comes from the Spanish word for "heights."

ALVARADO ROW and **ALVARADO COURT**, among the first residential streets on campus, commemorate Juan Bautista Alvarado (1809–82), leader of the 1836 California Revolt against Mexican authority and centralization, and governor of Alta California, 1836–42. His grandfather (also Juan Bautista Alvarado) was a member of the Portolá expedition of 1769. David Starr Jordan chose the name. According to Ellen Coit Elliott, Jordan originally called it Alvarado Avenue. However, he changed it to Alvarado Row because a row of pattern-book faculty houses lined the street, and, as she told him, "it is so obviously a row!" The road originally ended near the Quad's southeast corner.

★ **ANDREAS AVENUE** was presumably named after the San Andreas fault, which runs through the foothills to the south and west of the university, or for San Andreas Lake (1875) near Cañada de Raymundo in nearby San Mateo County. Located between Reservoir Drive and a part of what was then called Cabrillo Street (now part of Santa Ynez Street), Andreas Avenue became a spur of Mirada Avenue. San Andreas is a variant of San Andres, the Spanish name for the apostle Saint Andrew.

ANGELL COURT, in Escondido Village, honors Frank P. Angell (1857–1939), professor of psychology from 1892 to 1939. He was a graduate of the University of Vermont

(B.S., 1878) and the University of Leipzig (Ph.D., 1891). His scholarly publications included studies in the perception of time, such as *Experiments on the Discrimination of Clangs for Different Intervals of Time*. An early volunteer after the outbreak of World War I, Angell was a special representative to the Commission on Relief for Belgium (1915–16). Angell Field recognizes his service as chairman of the faculty committee on athletics, and his long-standing efforts on behalf of Stanford athletes.

★ **ANZA** †, a short street, met Granada [Road] and connected Lomita Drive and the old Mayfield Avenue. It was named for the Spanish explorer Captain Juan Bautista de Anza (1735–88), who led an expedition that opened an overland route to Alta California from Mexico. In 1776, Anza led another expedition that explored the San Francisco Bay Area.

ARBORETUM ROAD owes its name and location to Leland Stanford's vision of an arboretum. As early as 1880, Stanford spoke of his intention "to procure from all parts of the globe" every tree likely to succeed in California soil. Under this plan, 300 to 450 acres of parkland, along with the newly completed Arizona Garden and an already well-established vineyard, would surround Leland and Jane Stanford's proposed new man-

Frank P. Angell

sion on their Palo Alto Farm. Thousands of trees had been planted when the Stanfords' plans for the site changed following the death of Leland Jr. Although the arboretum was included in the new university's design, resources were largely devoted to completing buildings and developing the academic program. Fast-growing eucalyptus, planted to shade other more tender tree species, came to dominate the area.

ARGUELLO WAY, one of the earliest campus streets, runs (albeit discontinuously) parallel to Galvez Street. The name honors a distinguished family of Californios. José Darío Argüello, *comandante* of the presidios at San Francisco and Monterey, was governor of Alta California in 1814. His son, Luis Antonio, also a *comandante* at San Francisco, was the first native-born governor of Alta California, 1822–24. Perhaps, in selecting the name, President Jordan also recognized the significance of the Argüellos as local landowners. As early as the 1820s, the family claimed Rancho de las Pulgas (roughly present-day Menlo Park). Luis's widow, Maria Soledad Ortega de Argüello, battled squatters long after her property title was confirmed by the U.S. government in 1852.

AVERY MALL runs along the southeast side of the Avery Aquatic Center in the athletics complex. This facility, an expansion and renovation of the original DeGuerre complex of pools and courts, was made possible by a major gift from Burt and Marion "Pete" Avery and their family. Their four sons competed in swimming and water polo at Stanford. Burt is the only person ever to receive letters in football and rugby from both Stanford and the University of California. After completing under-graduate education at Berkeley, he graduated from Stanford's Graduate School of Business in 1948.

Subsequently, he worked as an engineer, founding the Avery Construction Company.

AYRSHIRE FARM LANE roughly parallels Bowdoin Street, off Campus Drive East. It marks the location of the Ayrshire Dairy Farm developed by Peter Coutts on his Matadero Rancho between 1875 and 1881. The 1,400-acre farm was stocked with Ayrshire and Holstein cattle. Leland Stanford purchased the land in 1882.

BARNES COURT, in Escondido Village, was presumably named for Earl Barnes (1861–1935), Stanford's first professor of education and secretary to the faculty (1891–97). He headed the Department of the History and Art of Education, precursor to the School of Education, and opened the first school for faculty children. His scholarly activity centered on the role of women and children in society, and on early childhood education. It may also be named for his wife, history professor Mary Sheldon Barnes (1850–98), the first woman appointed to the faculty; from 1892 to 1897, she taught an innovative course on Pacific Slope history.

BLACKWELDER COURT, in Escondido Village, is named for Eliot Blackwelder (1880–1969), who came to Stanford in 1922 as professor and chairman of geology. A gradu-

Earl Barnes

Mary Sheldon Barnes

ate at the University of Chicago (B.A., 1901), Blackwelder studied classics before turning to geology in his senior year. Before completing his Ph.D. (1914) at Chicago, he had become a full professor at the University of Wisconsin. He headed the geology department at the University of Illinois from 1916 to 1919. A member of the National Academy of Sciences, Blackwelder is noted for his extensive study of the geology of North America. He retired from Stanford in 1945.

BLAKE WILBUR DRIVE, off Pasteur Drive on the west side of Stanford Hospital, is named for Blake Wilbur (1901–73), son of university president Ray Lyman Wilbur. Blake Wilbur grew up on campus and earned his A.B. from Stanford in 1922 and his M.D. from Harvard in 1925. Dr. Wilbur was a clinical professor at the Stanford Medical School from 1930 to 1966. He was also a founder of the Palo Alto Medical Clinic (1930), and was affiliated with it for 40 years.

BONAIR SIDING serves the corporation yard area. The name appears on early maps showing the railroad spur built to deliver materials for construction of the original Quad. Until about 1910, Bonair served as a Southern Pacific Railroad stop between San Francisco and San Jose. Although the provenance of the name "Bonair"

Eliot Blackwelder   Blake Wilbur

for this location is unknown, *The Official Guide of the Railways and Steam Navigation Lines of the United States, Porto [sic] Rico, Canada, Mexico and Cuba* (1906) lists nine railway stations nationwide named Bonair, Bon Air, or Bonaire.

BOWDOIN STREET is an extension of a street in College Terrace (a section of Palo Alto), where all the streets are named for colleges and universities. Bowdoin College, in Brunswick, Maine, was founded in 1794. College Terrace was subdivided in 1888 and annexed to the town of Mayfield in 1891. Mayfield, in turn, was annexed to Palo Alto in 1925.

★ **BRANNER AVENUE** extended from Salvatierra Street to Escondido Road, parallel to Arguello. It was named for John Casper Branner (1850–1922), Stanford's second president (1913–15). Branner was working as state geologist of Arkansas when David Starr Jordan recruited him to Stanford in 1891. Branner received his B.S. from Cornell in 1882 and Ph.D. from Indiana University in 1885, where he began his academic career. At Stanford, he was chairman of the Geology Department for 23 years, and university vice president from 1898 to 1913. He was an authority on South American geology, especially that of Brazil, and was well known for his surveys

John Casper Branner

of the western United States for the U.S. Geological Survey. As a special state commissioner on the San Francisco earthquake of 1906, he surveyed damage along the San Andreas fault. In 1916, President Woodrow Wilson appointed him to investigate the cause of massive landslides affecting operations of the Panama Canal.

BUCKEYE LANE, one of several campus streets named for a California native tree, is a short service road west of Schwab Residential Center that leads to a cluster of dormitories and eating clubs. The name refers to the California buckeye (*Aesculus californica*).

CABRILLO STREET, on San Juan Hill, is named for Juan Rodríguez Cabrillo, a Portuguese navigator in the service of Spain. In 1542, he commanded an expedition that sailed up the coast of California about as far north as Monterey. Though he gave Spanish names to many significant locations, the names have not survived. The Spanish did little with Cabrillo's discoveries until the 1700s. Cabrillo Street's designation has changed over time. It once comprised a portion of what is now Santa Ynez Street. At that time, Santa Ynez ran straight uphill to Reservoir Drive. Together, Cabrillo and Dolores Streets enclosed Reservoir Drive; they met at the midpoint of Andreas Avenue.

CAMPUS DRIVE is a belt road circling the main campus. It has two sections, EAST and WEST, each connecting Palm Drive to Junipero Serra Boulevard. A significant portion of the eastern portion of the road was first constructed in the 1960s to divert auto traffic away from the central academic and residential areas surrounding the Quad.

★ **CAPISTRANO** † branched westward from Anza, toward the front of the Knoll. It was named for Mission San Juan Capistrano.

CASANUEVA PLACE, a cul-de-sac in the Pine Hill II residential subdivision, may be named for Francisco Casanueva, a native of Chile who became a San Francisco attorney. Between 1851 and 1854, he secured a deed to the entire San Francisquito Rancho, a portion of which is now the site of the Stanford campus.

CATHCART WAY, in the Frenchman's Hill residential subdivision, is named for Arthur Martin Cathcart (1873–1949), a member of the Stanford class of 1896. From 1904 until his retirement in 1938, he taught constitutional law and torts at Stanford. A.M. Cathcart was active in university governance, serving many years on the executive committee of the Academic Council and on the Advisory Board. He served on the Palo Alto City Council from 1918 to 1936 and was mayor from 1920 to 1924.

CEDRO WAY, in the Pine Hill II residential subdivision, takes its name from the Spanish word for "cedar." In Stanford's early days, a residence across San Francisquito Creek was known as Cedro Cottage. Originally, it was the home of Ariel Lathrop, a brother

Arthur Martin Cathcart

of Jane Stanford and manager of the Stanfords' Palo Alto Farm from 1880 to 1892. Later residents included Professor Oliver P. Jenkins and Professor Thorstein Veblen, author of *The Theory of the Leisure Class* (1899) and the economist who coined the term conspicuous consumption. (The plot of land, formerly owned by the university, today is the site of Menlo Park's Oak Knoll elementary school.)

CHARLES MARX WAY, in the Stanford West Apartments subdivision, is named for pioneer faculty member Charles David Marx (1857–1939), first head of the Civil Engineering Department. Known familiarly as "Daddy," Marx was a genial and forceful teacher and an influential voice in campus affairs. He received his bachelor's degree at Cornell (1878) and later studied in Europe. A member of the 1906 team of engineers who investigated campus earthquake damage and supervised reconstruction, Marx and colleagues C.B. Wing and William F. Durand later designed Stanford Stadium. Professor Marx also was involved in Palo Alto civic affairs. Except for 1904–08, from 1896 to 1933 he served on the town's Board of Trustees and later its City Council.

CHURCHILL MALL runs through a complex of playing fields near El Camino Real. It is a slightly offset exten-

Charles David Marx

sion of Palo Alto's Churchill Avenue. According to *Streets of Palo Alto*, that street owes its name to the American novelist Winston Churchill (1871–1947), not the British statesman. The novelist (no relation) was born in St. Louis and educated at the U.S. Naval Academy. His early books were historical novels, including *The Celebrity* (1898) and *Richard Carvel* (1899); the latter sold nearly a million copies. Later novels focused on political, religious, and social problems. Churchill served in the New Hampshire legislature and was a Progressive candidate for the governorship.

CLARK WAY, in the Stanford West Apartments subdivision, honors graphic art professor Arthur Bridgeman Clark (1866–1948). Clark earned his B.A. at Syracuse University in 1888 and M.A. in 1891. There, he was an instructor in architecture and also was a drawing instructor and director of the trade school at Elmira (New York) State Reformatory. In 1892, David Starr Jordan recruited him to Stanford. With Professor Bolton Brown, he founded the Department of Art and Architecture, and became its first chairman. Clark settled in the College Terrace neighborhood of Mayfield, playing a leading role in incorporation of the town and was its first mayor. The Clarks' four children were Birge, a noted local architect; Esther, the Peninsula's

Arthur Bridgeman Clark

first pediatrician and a founding partner of the Palo Alto Medical Clinic; and twins Donald, a chemical engineer; and David, also an architect.

COMSTOCK CIRCLE is named after John Henry Comstock (1849–1931), a professor of entomology at Cornell University who, at the request of President Jordan, established the Department of Entomology at Stanford. From 1891 to 1900, he taught at Stanford during January, February, and March, his vacation period from Cornell. Comstock retired from Cornell in 1914. The street is located in Escondido Village.

CONSTANZO STREET, on San Juan Hill, is named for Miguel Constanzo (1741–1814), a military engineer and cosmographer who, in 1769, accompanied Gaspar de Portolá on the first land expedition to Alta California. He later designed the presidios of San Diego, Monterey, San Francisco, and Santa Barbara. In history books, his surname is usually given as *Costansó*. Publication of his diary, *El descubrimiento de la Bahia de San Francisco: la expedición de Portolá de 1769–1770,* the first book that relates exclusively to California, was initially suppressed in Mexico because it was thought to give too much information to the British.

John Henry Comstock

COOKSEY LANE is named after George B. Cooksey and his wife, Linda Dows Cooksey, who were friends of Jane Stanford. In 1900, the Cookseys were permitted by Mrs. Stanford to build a large house on San Juan Hill, one of the few private (non-Stanford) residences allowed on campus. Their residence later became a fraternity house, Phi Kappa Psi. It is now Synergy House.

★ **COOKSEY ROAD** was a lane extending from Costanso (the original, correct spelling of today's Constanzo) to San Juan, at roughly a right angle to today's Cooksey Lane.

CORONADO AVENUE is a short street running from Mayfield Avenue to just beyond Alvarado Row. It was the southernmost street of the original campus residential area and was named for Francisco Vásquez de Coronado (1510–54), a famous Spanish explorer of the American Southwest.

COTTRELL WAY curves through the Frenchman's Hill residential subdivision and has two intersections with Raimundo Way. The street is named for Edwin Angell Cottrell (1881–1953), a graduate of Swarthmore (A.B., 1907) and Harvard (A.M., 1919). He was at Stanford from

Edwin Angell Cottrell

1919 to 1953. He was professor and co-founder of the Department of Political Science and from 1927 to 1945 served as its head. He was active in university governance and community affairs and in 1924 became mayor of Palo Alto, succeeding another Stanford professor, Arthur Cathcart.

COWELL LANE provides access to Lane C from Campus Drive East. It ran alongside the Cowell Student Health Center (now demolished and replaced by the Vaden Health Center), which was built with a gift from the S.H. Cowell Foundation. The foundation also provided funds for numerous other health centers around the country. Samuel Henry Cowell (1862–1955) was the son of Henry Cowell (1819–1925), who came to California from New England during the Gold Rush. The Cowell family's financial interests in Northern California and the state of Washington included limestone quarries, cement mills, timber lands, ranches, and commercial buildings.

CROTHERS WAY is named for George Edward Crothers (1870–1951), a prominent Stanford alumnus (1895) and benefactor. He played a crucial role in correcting legal defects in the Founding Grant and obtaining tax-exempt status for Stanford lands dedicated to educational purposes. A member of Stanford's first graduating class

George Edward Crothers

(1895), Crothers was the first alumnus elected to the Board of Trustees (1902–12). An influential lawyer, he served as judge of San Francisco Superior Court, 1913–20, and was active in California Progressive politics, fostering significant reforms in state labor and banking laws, and women's suffrage. Crothers Way is a service road that runs between Encina Commons and Crothers and Crothers Memorial residential halls; from there it extends to a point behind the East Wing of Green Library. Automotive access is from Arguello Way, just off Serra Street.

DOLORES STREET, on San Juan Hill, is named after Mission Dolores, the popular title for Mission San Francisco de Asís. The mission, completed in 1791, is in San Francisco on a site adjacent to a stream that the Spanish explorer Juan Bautista de Anza called *Arroyo de los Dolores* ("stream of sorrows").

DUDLEY LANE, in Escondido Village, is named for William Russell Dudley (1849–1911), a professor of botany and a Cornell classmate of President Jordan. He received his A.B. in 1874, M.S. in 1876, and studied in Europe before joining the Cornell faculty, where he served until recruited to Stanford in 1892. He was an expert on California flora, well known for his long hikes through the rugged

William Russell Dudley

Coastal Range and Sierra Nevada, and was an influential advocate for conservation of the redwoods. Following his unexpected death, in 1911, the large collection of botanical specimens he and his colleagues had assembled was named the Dudley Herbarium. In 1976, the collection's 650,000 specimens were merged into those of the California Academy of Sciences in San Francisco.

DUENA STREET runs behind the Old Union. *Dueña* is Spanish for a female owner or landlady. The word also means "pay office" and may have to do with the nearby living quarters for workmen who built the Quad. In 1892, those barracks were taken over by students—many with literary talents—who renamed them The Camp. They were used as lodgings until they were demolished in 1902.

DURAND WAY, in the Stanford West Apartments subdivision, is named for mechanical engineering Professor William Frederick Durand (1859–1958). He was an 1880 graduate of the U.S. Naval Academy at Annapolis and received his Ph.D. from Lafayette College in 1888. He served on the Cornell faculty from 1891 to 1904, when he was appointed head of Stanford's Mechanical Engineering Department, a position he held until his retirement in 1924. He served on many university com-

William Frederick Durand

mittees, including the 1906 earthquake commission, and on many government advisory boards. Durand is known for his work on marine and airplane propellers, as well as his contributions to the technology of jet propulsion. He was the recipient of many awards and honors, including the Wright Brothers Memorial Trophy in 1948. Durand, who lived to be nearly 100, offered this advice for a long life: "Have interesting work, eat wisely, get a good night's rest every night, and don't worry."

EL CAMINO REAL is Spanish for "The Royal Road." This busy thoroughfare runs along the northeasterly edge of the campus. More generally, El Camino Real is the name given to the pathway connecting the missions of Alta California established by the Franciscans in the late 18th and early 19th centuries. Several pathways were followed up the Peninsula during the mission days, depending on seasonal conditions. Through the later 19th century and early 20th century, the section of this street separating Stanford and Palo Alto was called the San Francisco–San Jose Road or The County Road. Its designation as El Camino Real did not occur until about 100 years ago.

ELECTIONEER ROAD connects Campus Drive West to Fremont Road, site of the historic Stock Farm and Red

Electioneer, champion trotter

Barn. It was named in 1985 to commemorate the trotting champion Electioneer, whose statue can be found there. This animal, bought by Governor Stanford in 1876 for $12,000, was called the "world champion sire of world champions." In 14 years at Palo Alto, he sired 9 of Stanford's 19 world champions and 166 colts that could trot the mile in less than 2 minutes 30 seconds. A kiosk explaining the history of Leland Stanford's Stock Farm is located near the statue. (See STOCK FARM ROAD.)

EL ESCARPADO WAY is a short cul-de-sac off Gerona Road. The name is derived from the Spanish word for "escarpment" or "steep slope."

ESCONDIDO ROAD leads to and takes its name from a large cottage, originally the home of Peter Coutts. The cottage later became the first campus residence of David Starr Jordan, who named it Escondite Cottage. *Escondite* is Spanish for "hideaway" or "hideout," as in the game of hide-and-seek. The word *escondido,* on the other hand, means "hidden" (often in the context of a body of water). Partly a pedestrian mall and partly a street for vehicular traffic, Escondido traverses the campus from Lomita Mall to Stanford Avenue, passing through Escondido Village. It was first named Portola Street and ran from Lomita to Lasuen, directly behind the Quad.

ESPLANADA WAY is a street in the Pine Hill I residential subdivision. The Spanish word *esplanada* means "esplanade" (an English word adopted from French), a level stretch of paved or grassy ground, especially one used for walking or driving along a shore. In this case, there is no visible shore, but a creek not far away may have served the purpose.

ESTUDILLO ROAD connects Frenchman's Road and
Lathrop Drive in the Pine Hill II faculty residential subdi-
vision. It appears to have been named for José María
Estudillo, a military officer attached to the Monterey
Presidio. At one time Estudillo was comandante of the
San Diego Presidio.

★ **EUCALYPTUS ROAD** is the name used until 1990 for
what is now called Nelson Road and Mel Nelson Mall.
Hundreds of eucalyptus trees are abundant in the nearby arboretum area. (See NELSON ROAD.)

★ **FLORES** † is another name mentioned by David Starr
Jordan in his autobiography, *The Days of a Man. Flores*
(Spanish for "flowers") is a fairly common surname.
The Flores in question may have been José Maria
Flores, a Mexican general and briefly leader of Alta
California after the 1846 flight of Pío Pico (the last
Mexican governor of Alta California) to Sonora. Another
Flores (Juan) was a noted outlaw. Still another
(Teodoro) is mentioned in the Last Will and Testament
of Rafael Soto, the owner of Rancho Rinconada del
Arroyo de San Francisquito, a land grant on which
much of Palo Alto now stands. The precise location
of this street, if it ever really existed, is unknown.

FOOTHILL ROAD is a name used at various times for all or
part of today's Junipero Serra Boulevard. The foothills of
the Santa Cruz Mountains lie just to the south and west
of this county road, but to judge from old maps, it is diffi-
cult to fix the precise extent of Foothill Road. A campus
map of 1928 identifies the portion of today's Junipero
Serra Boulevard—between what were then called
Coronado Avenue and Alturas Drive—as Foothill Road,
even though the two other segments between Santa
Cruz Avenue (in Menlo Park) and Page Mill Road were

labeled as Junipero Serra Boulevard. Sometimes Foothill Road was applied locally to the entirety of Junipero Serra Boulevard. The name Foothill Road ceased to be used about 1965, when Foothill Expressway from Page Mill Road to Cupertino was constructed.

FREMONT ROAD runs perpendicular to Electioneer Road near the western edge of the main campus. Formerly linked to Junipero Serra Boulevard, this little-known Stanford street was presumably named for John Charles Frémont (1813–80), a major figure in California history. He was born in Savannah, Georgia, the son of a French immigrant. As a lieutenant in the Army Corps of Topographical Engineers, he explored Oregon and Northern California and is noted for his involvement in the Bear Flag Revolt against California's Mexican government in 1846. Published reports of his expeditions were an important source of information for Americans coming overland, especially during the Gold Rush. In 1850–51, he served as a U.S. senator from California, and in 1856, he ran as the Republican Party's first presidential candidate, losing to James Buchanan. Frémont was appointed a major general in 1861 by Abraham Lincoln and served as military governor of occupied Missouri, but was removed from office after freeing Missouri's slaves (occupied border states were not included in Lincoln's Emancipation Proclamation). Thereafter, his military and political fortunes declined considerably. In Thompson and West's *Historical Atlas Map of Santa Clara County* (1876), the northwest corner of the county—including present-day Stanford, Palo Alto, Mountain View, and Los Altos—was named Frémont township.

★ **FRENCH LAKE DRIVE** was a name for the segment of Frenchman's Road from Mayfield Avenue to the "County Road," which became Gerona Road. At one time it was also called "Coronado" or "Coronada." The name refers to Frenchman's Lake, a reservoir constructed nearby by Peter Coutts, the Mysterious Frenchman. (See PETER COUTTS ROAD.)

FRENCHMAN'S ROAD runs between Mayfield Avenue and Junipero Serra Boulevard, where it now dead-ends. The Frenchman for whom this street is named was Peter Coutts, who established Matadero Rancho in 1875. The road once led to a manmade lake lined with trees and various brick structures, of which only a few vestiges remain today. (See PETER COUTTS ROAD.)

GALVEZ STREET is named for José de Gálvez (1720–87), who in 1765 was appointed inspector general of New Spain, i.e., Mexico. In 1767, he implemented a royal decree expelling the Jesuits from New Spain. The following year, King Carlos III ordered him to Baja California. There, Gálvez appointed Gaspar de Portolá as military commander of the Alta California expedition and Junípero Serra, a Franciscan missionary, as the expedition's religious leader.

GERONA ROAD takes its name from a province in northeast Spain bounded by the Mediterranean Sea to the east and France to the north. The western end of Gerona Road was once known as Alturas Drive. (*Alturas* is the Spanish word for "heights.") Gerona at one time connected to Foothill Road.

GOVERNOR'S AVENUE was once a 1.4-mile-long eucalyptus-lined lane that ran from the Stanford residence near San Francisquito Creek to the reservoir (Lagunita), then turned sharply to the barns and paddocks of the Palo Alto Stock Farm's trotting department. The lane, planted in the 1870s with more than 700 Tasmanian blue gums (*Eucalyptus globulus*), appears on old maps as Gum Tree Lane and Governor's Lane. The latter commemorates this favorite drive of Leland Stanford, who served as governor of California during the Civil War. Interestingly, Governor's Avenue is aligned true north, whereas Palm Drive is magnetic north. Only a small section of the road, not far from Governor's Corner, remains. Most of the trees have succumbed to old age, drought, severe freezes, and development, but specimens can still be seen on the remnant of road near Santa Teresa Street and part of Panama Street.

★ **GRANADA** † is a city and a province in Spain, the birthplace of Don Antonio de Mendoza (see MENDOZA [road]). Granada is also a city in Nicaragua, the country that Leland Stanford crossed en route to California in 1852. The short stump of a street between residences now named Grove-Lasuen and the Robert Moore houses ("BOB" and Casa Italiana) once connected Lasuen Street to Mayfield Avenue. It eventually was absorbed, with part of Mayfield Avenue, into Campus Drive East.

HOSKINS COURT is situated in Escondido Village, just off Serra Street. The street is named for early faculty member Leander Miller Hoskins (1860–1937), a professor of applied mathematics and author of books on

Governor Leland Stanford

hydrostatics, hydraulics, and theoretical mechanics. Hoskins received his degrees from the University of Wisconsin, where he joined the faculty and rose from instructor in engineering to professor of theoretical and applied mechanics. He came to Stanford in 1892, and retired in 1925.

HULME COURT, in Escondido Village, is named for Edward Maslin Hulme (1871–1951), a professor of history who received his A.B. degree at Stanford (1897) and his A.M. at Cornell (1902). He was a University Scholar at Harvard (1900–01) and also studied at the Sorbonne in Paris. He joined Stanford's History Department in 1921, specializing in religious history of Europe in the Middle Ages and Renaissance. Hulme, a popular lecturer, was noted for his wide range of interests, which, besides history, included literature and the arts. He retired in 1937.

JENKINS COURT is an Escondido Village street commemorating Oliver Peebles Jenkins (1850–1935), a professor of physiology and histology. He received his M.S. in 1886 and Ph.D. in 1889 at Indiana University. A member of Stanford's pioneer faculty, Jenkins taught at Stanford from 1891 until his retirement, in 1916. He was a cofounder, with Charles Gilbert, of the Hopkins

Leander Miller Hoskins

Edward Maslin Hulme

Oliver Peebles Jenkins

Seaside Laboratory in Pacific Grove (today's Hopkins Marine Station). The Jenkinses were the first faculty family to occupy Cedro Cottage, the former home of Ariel Lathrop, a brother of Mrs. Stanford.

★ **JORDAN AVENUE**, named for David Starr Jordan, the university's first president, ran from Branner Avenue to Arguello Way (which originally was much longer than it is today). This street is not to be confused with Jordan Way.

JORDAN WAY, just off Campus Drive West near Jordan Quad, is named for Stanford's first president, David Starr Jordan (1851–1931). Educated at Cornell (M.S., 1872), Jordan held a number of teaching positions in the natural sciences before becoming professor of biology at Butler College (1875–79), professor of zoology at Indiana University (1879–85), then president of Indiana University in 1885. Known for his advocacy of higher education, he enthusiastically accepted Leland Stanford's offer of the presidency, despite the prospect of heading an institution whose sole "trustee" was one of California's most powerful businessmen and politicians. Jordan successfully balanced the intentions of Leland and Jane Stanford with the needs of a growing faculty and student body. His personality dominated the

David Starr Jordan

campus through economic troubles during the 1890s, a growth spurt after 1899, the devastation of the 1906 earthquake, and subsequent new academic directions. A renowned lecturer and prolific author, he also balanced his ongoing scientific interests, particularly ichthyology, and his participation in civic and political reform, with his presidential duties. An ardent pacifist, he retired in 1913 to devote his time to the world peace movement. That year, he was named chancellor of the university. Jordan Way is near the site of the original location of Jordan's residence, Serra House, which was later moved across campus.

JUNIPERO SERRA BOULEVARD, a county road running behind the central campus and Lagunita, connects Page Mill and Alpine Roads, and includes a portion called Foothill Road until the 1960s. The street is named for Father Serra, the founder of nine California missions. (See SERRA STREET and FOOTHILL ROAD.)

LAGUNITA DRIVE runs toward Lagunita and terminates near the site where the third Stanford Boathouse once stood. (It was demolished in 1989 because of its hazardous condition.) Lagunita refers to the "little lake," a 115-million-gallon irrigation reservoir built by Leland Stanford in 1878–79 to serve his Palo Alto Stock Farm. Named by President Jordan, the lake is often mislabeled "Lake Lagunita," which translates "Lake Little Lake."

LANE A once ran through the first residential area, between Salvatierra and what was then Lasuen. Only the northerly portion of Lane A remains by that name; it is a service road from the west end of Nathan Abbott Way, between the Law School and the Post Office, and up to the loading dock of the Stanford Bookstore, where it dead-ends. A middle section of the old Lane A was located where today's Pearce Mitchell Place is found. The southerly end of the original Lane A became Valparaiso Street.

LANE B is an alley that runs from Campus Drive East to Coronado Avenue. Like its counterparts, Lanes A, C, and W, this road was part of the design created by the university's original planner and landscape architect, Frederick Law Olmsted. (See OLMSTED ROAD.)

LANE C is another alley that runs between Campus Drive East and Coronado Avenue. Having bollards at both ends, it no longer serves as a through street but more of a bike and pedestrian path as well as a service road. Automotive access to Lane C is from Cowell Lane, off Campus Drive East.

LANE L runs behind Lagunita Court and Roble Hall.

LANE W once was a through street, but now is a cul-de-sac that runs off Mayfield Avenue, behind student residences Xanadu, Casa Italiana, and "BOB."

LASUEN STREET, named by David Starr Jordan, commemorates Father Fermin Francisco de Lasuén (1736–1803). Leaving Spain in 1759, he served at Franciscan missions in Mexico, including one in Baja California. From there he traveled with Father Palóu by land to San Diego. Lasuén founded numerous missions in Alta California, and succeeded Father Junípero Serra as their head. The street proper begins at the rear of the Littlefield Center, running parallel to Palm Drive and continuing north across Campus Drive East to Arboretum Road. As a pedestrian mall, Lasuen runs from Littlefield Center across Serra Mall and along the east side of the Quad to White Plaza, then past Braun Music Center and several Row houses to Mayfield Avenue. Lasuen originally extended to present-day Campus Drive West; that segment is now part of Mayfield. Pedestrians began replacing cars on Lasuen in the 1960s.

LATHROP DRIVE and **LATHROP PLACE**, in the Pine Hill residential area, honor university co-founder Jane Lathrop Stanford (1828–1905) and her brothers. Mrs. Stanford was a driving force behind the development of the university. Initially interested primarily in the Leland Stanford Junior Museum and in construction of Memorial Church, she took on duties as sole trustee at the age of 65, following the death of her husband in 1893, until her retirement in 1903. Older brother Ariel Lathrop served as manager of the Stanford family's Palo Alto estate from 1880 to 1892. He was succeeded by the youngest Lathrop sibling, Charles, who also was university treasurer. Another younger brother, Henry Clay, lived at Mrs. Stanford's home as an invalid until his death in 1900. He is buried near the Stanford Family Mausoleum beneath the Angel of Grief.

LINKS ROAD is an appropriate name for a street that leads to the clubhouse of a golf course, and that is exactly what this one does. The street, an extension

Ariel Lathrop

Charles Lathrop

Henry Clay Lathrop

of Campus Drive West, goes up the hillside south of Junipero Serra Boulevard to the clubhouse.

LOMITA DRIVE is an original campus street that once permitted access to the west side of the Quad—the east side being entered by Lasuen Street. *Lomita* is Spanish for "little hill." One section of Lomita Drive begins at Campus Drive West and runs parallel to Palm Drive toward the Quad. The other section runs from Santa Teresa Street to The Knoll (originally Cemetery Hill and later the mansion built for Ray Lyman Wilbur as the president's residence, 1919–43). **LOMITA COURT** is an extension providing access to fraternity clusters and housing units in that area.

LOS ARBOLES AVENUE is a short residential street just off Santa Teresa Street, running parallel to Campus Drive West. The name is Spanish for "the trees." It was originally an access road, leading from Searsville Road on campus along the golf course to Foothill Road (today's Junipero Serra Boulevard). It was cut off in the 1960s, and later bypassed and replaced by Campus Drive West.

MARX WAY, see **CHARLES MARX WAY**

Jane Lathrop Stanford

MASTERS MALL honors Alfred R. Masters (1898–1963). The street runs alongside Masters Grove, a recreational area near Churchill Mall in the athletic complex. Masters was student body president (1923–24) and captain of the soccer team. Following his graduation with a bachelor's degree in geology (1924), he returned to his birthplace, Portland, Oregon, where he spent a year in private business. In 1925 he returned to Stanford as graduate manager, later general manager, of the Board of Athletic Control (BAC), created in 1916 to oversee campus athletics. Until athletics were interrupted by World War II, the BAC was a very successful operation. From 1943 to 1946, Masters served as assistant controller. He was appointed Stanford's first director of athletics in 1946. He was noted for his pioneering developments in sports broadcasting and his tireless promotion of Stanford athletics.

MAYFIELD AVENUE refers to the town of Mayfield, which was established in 1867 and annexed to Palo Alto in 1925. The town got its name from the Mayfield Farm established in 1853 by Elisha Crosby, a member of California's constitutional convention and an early state senator. Within its borders, Mayfield included a portion of Peter Coutts's farm, today's College Terrace, and a strip of land between El Camino Real and the railroad

Alfred R. Masters

lines. Unlike the young town of Palo Alto, Mayfield was not "dry." Indeed, "The Road to Mayfield," a popular student drinking song of the 1890s, refers to the pleasures of its many saloons. In the 1880s, the original Mayfield-Searsville Road traversed the Stanford estate, roughly following today's Escondido Road, Searsville Road, and Searsville Path, but was blocked by early construction of the Quadrangle in 1889–90; it joined the town of Mayfield and the now-lost community of Searsville, located in the foothills near Jasper Ridge. (See SEARSVILLE ROAD.)

McDONALD MALL, see **SAM McDONALD MALL**

McFARLAND COURT in Escondido Village is named for Frank Mace MacFarland (1869–1951), professor of histology, who first joined the faculty as an instructor in 1892. (He allowed his name to be spelled both ways in official university documents.) MacFarland received his B.A. from DePauw (1889), A.M. from Stanford (1893), and Ph.D. from the University of Würzburg (1896). An authority on marine mollusks, he played a major role in the organization of Hopkins Marine Station and in the development of the California Academy of Sciences. MacFarland was president of the academy for 14 years, and after retiring from teaching in 1934 was acting

Frank Mace MacFarland

director of its museum and Steinhart Aquarium in San
Francisco. A beautifully colored sea slug, *Chromodoris
macfarlandi,* is named in his honor.

MEARS COURT, off Stanford Avenue in the Frenchman's
Hill residential subdivision, is named for Eliot Grinnell
Mears (1889–1946), who joined the Economics Depart-
ment in 1921, later shifted to the Graduate School of
Business as professor of geography and international
trade. His maternal grandfather, Josiah Bushnell Grinnell
(to whom Horace Greeley gave the famous advice, "Go
West, young man"), founded Grinnell, Iowa. As a Harvard
undergraduate, Eliot Mears was editor of the *Harvard
Lampoon.* He earned a B.A. in 1910 and an M.B.A. there
in 1912. In 1919, Mears served as economic member of the
American Military Mission to Armenia and Transylvania.

MEDICAL LANE is a very short street leading from
Campus Drive West into the Medical Center parking lot.

MEDICAL WAY, an extension of Roth Way, leads to the
Medical Center from Campus Drive West.

★ **MENDOZA** † was named for Don Antonio de
Mendoza (c. 1490–1552), first viceroy of New Spain.

—*continued on page 43*

Eliot Grinnell Mears

By 1913, Sand Hill Road showed more tire marks than wagon ruts.

The map at right appeared in the
Stanford Bulletin of 1956, before the
subsequent burst of automotive traffic
and building activity beginning in the 1960s.
The network of campus roadways shown here
differs markedly from what we have today,
most significantly in the absence
of a ring road, Campus Drive. Other notable
differences include the names and lengths
of some streets; among these are
Foothill Road, Mayfield Avenue, Lasuen Street,
Arguello Street, Panama Street, and
Pine Avenue. This map reflects the
long-standing community perspective
of moving up Palm Drive to the Quad, rather
than the university's more recent policy of
orienting campus maps with north at the top.

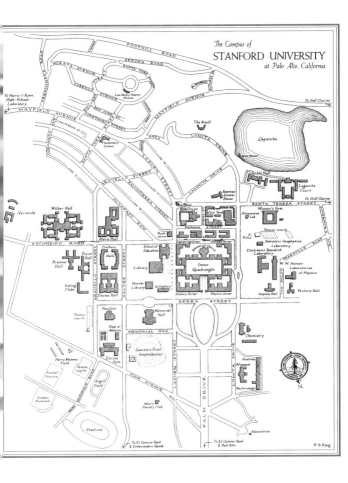

The Campus of
STANFORD UNIVERSITY
at Palo Alto, California

P.S. King

Quiet along the Row: Kappa Kappa Gamma and neighbors on Lasuen (now a portion of Mayfield Avenue) in the 1920s.

—*continued from page 38*

This street ran between Anza and Lomita Avenue, now Lomita Drive, today a short distance northwest of Campus Drive East.

MIRADA AVENUE takes its name from the Spanish word meaning "glance" or "gaze." Located on San Juan Hill, this street boasts the Hoover House, built in 1919 by Lou Henry Hoover ('98) and Herbert Hoover ('95) and, since 1944, official residence of Stanford's president.

MORRIS WAY see **SAMUEL MORRIS WAY**

MOSHER WAY, in the Stanford West Apartments sub-division, honors Clelia Duel Mosher (1863–1940), a graduate of Stanford (A.B., 1893; A.M., 1894) and of Johns Hopkins Medical School (M.D., 1900). Dr. Mosher was an authority on women's health and physiology, although she is best remembered for her pioneering study of sexual attitudes of 45 women, conducted while practicing medicine in Palo Alto. (This research antici-pated the Kinsey report by 50 years.) She returned to campus in 1910 as assistant professor of personal hygiene and medical advisor to women. During World War I, she served in France as medical investigator for the Children's Bureau and associate medical director

Clelia Duel Mosher

of the Bureau of Refugees and Relief of the American Red Cross. She resumed her duties at Stanford after the armistice and retired in 1929 with the rank of professor.

MUSEUM WAY lies between Lasuen Street and Lomita Drive, where the museum is sited. Leland Stanford Jr. was an avid collector and the museum, like the university, was established in his memory. Along with Memorial Church, the museum was a favorite project of Jane Stanford, who served as its de facto director and major donor of art and artifacts. The museum, which was badly damaged in the 1906 earthquake, later was renovated and reopened. The 1989 Loma Prieta earthquake damaged it severely; renovated and expanded, it reopened in 1999 as the Iris and B. Gerald Cantor Center for Visual Arts.

NATHAN ABBOTT WAY leads from Alvarado Row to the Law School building. After graduating from Boston University Law School, Nathan Abbott (1854–1941) came to Stanford in 1893 to establish the Department of Law. (The department did not grant graduate degrees until 1916; it became a school in 1926.) Abbott served as professor and head of the law faculty from 1893 until 1907, when he took a position at Columbia University.

Nathan Abbott

NELSON ROAD runs from Galvez Street to the parking lot between Stanford Stadium and Sunken Diamond. There it becomes MEL NELSON MALL and continues to the artificial turf fields. The road and mall are named for Melvin A. "Mel" Nelson (1910–89), who was hired as a groundskeeper in 1927 and given responsibility for the stadium. In 1962, he succeeded Sam McDonald as superintendent of athletic buildings and grounds (see SAM McDONALD MALL). Nelson retired after 50 years of service at Stanford. Before the road was renamed for him in 1990, it was called Eucalyptus Road.

NORTH SERVICE ROAD leads from Campus Drive West behind the Gates Building to the back of Herrin Hall and Laboratories. Its counterpart, South Service Road, has become a pedestrian mall.

NORTH-SOUTH MALL is a pedestrian artery linking several science and engineering buildings in the west campus area. At its northern extremity it is called the North-South Axis.

OAK ROAD is a west campus road named in 1985. It begins at Welch Road, crosses Stock Farm Road, and terminates at Searsville Road. The road passes a grassland area framed by stately oaks, some more than 200 years old.

Melvin A. "Mel" Nelson

OLMSTED ROAD is a nearly circumferential street in Escondido Village. It honors Frederick Law Olmsted (1822–1903), the celebrated landscape architect retained by the Stanfords in 1886 to develop the overall plan for the new university. As a young man, Olmsted had become famous for his design (in collaboration with British architect Calvert Vaux) of Central Park in New York City. In addition to his legacy of distinguished landscape architecture, Olmsted was noted for his out-spoken opposition to slavery. From 1852 to 1855, he reported weekly from the American South for the *New York Times.* This led to the publication of his important book *The Cotton Kingdom: A Traveler's Observations on Cotton and Slavery in the American Slave States* (1861).

PAGE MILL ROAD is named for William Page who, with Alexander Peers, owned a mill in the foothills west of the town of Searsville and a lumberyard in Mayfield. The road was used to bring logs from the mill to the lumberyard. The northern end of today's Page Mill Road begins at El Camino Real in what once was Mayfield. It then runs southward to the hills along the edge of Stanford's Peter Coutts and Frenchman's Hill faculty residential subdivisions. On the right, just beyond Junipero Serra Boulevard is Old Page Mill Road, a 1-mile stretch of the original roadway. In the town of

Frederick Law Olmsted

Mayfield, the road was once known as Washington Avenue and was the first of a series of parallel avenues named for famous Americans: Sheridan, Grant, Sherman, and Lincoln. (To avoid duplication of names when Palo Alto annexed Mayfield in 1925, Lincoln was renamed California Avenue.)

PALM DRIVE, the university's grand entry street, leads 3,750 feet from El Camino Real to the Oval, which lies below the Quadrangle. Originally named as a continuation of Palo Alto's University Avenue, this impressive street was lined with palm trees in 1893 at President Jordan's suggestion. Campus designer Frederick Law Olmsted positioned the road in the university plans in 1888 as "an avenue to a proposed railway station" (built soon after in the village of University Park, today's Palo Alto). In 1901, Jane Stanford forbade automobiles on campus, reserving Palm Drive for carriages, bicycles, and pedestrians. In 1908, all streets except Palm Drive were opened to automobiles. By 1914, when virtually no traffic was using Palm Drive, trustees lifted the car ban. In 1994, the road was completely rebuilt and resurfaced, and the granite curbs, called for in Olmsted's original plan, were finally added.

★ **PALO ALTO AVENUE** appears briefly, on the Sanborn Fire Insurance Map of 1924, as running from the intersection of present-day Lomita Drive and Lagunita Drive along the west side of the Quadrangle all the way to the vicinity of the Mausoleum. This route is now Lomita Drive and Lomita Mall.

PALO ROAD connects Palm Drive to Hoover Pavilion (formerly called Palo Alto Hospital). The street name comes from the Spanish for "stick." It is not far from the famous redwood tree, El Palo Alto, that inspired the name of Leland Stanford's Palo Alto Farm and, later, of the city of Palo Alto. It's unclear whether the tree designated in contemporary lore is the same one mentioned by Palou in 1774.

PAMPAS LANE runs from Serra Street to a service area that includes the Children's Center of the Stanford Community. The name of the street is Spanish for "prairie." Ellen Coit Elliott, wife of Stanford's first registrar, described the general area including this locale as a "plain running to the Bay [with] one or two ranch houses; otherwise mostly 'wheat field.'"

PANAMA STREET begins at Campus Drive West and, for a few hundred yards, covers the same ground as Governor's Avenue. After a 90° turn, it runs along what might have been the original Mayfield-Searsville Road. How and when the name was chosen are still unclear, although it appears not to have been used until around 1915. A plausible conjecture is that the name highlights the important role played by the Isthmus of Panama in the history of Gold Rush California as a popular shortcut bypassing Cape Horn. The opening of the Panama Canal in 1914 further simplified and speeded up the transcontinental journey. It is possible that San Francisco's Panama-Pacific Exposition in 1915 gave additional motivation for the naming of this street. Early maps of Stanford show that a portion of the Peninsula Railway's "Toonerville Trolley" line (1909–29) ran along what is now Panama Street, past Encina Hall, and down Galvez Street to Palo Alto.

PASTEUR DRIVE is the name chosen for the entry road to the Medical School and Hospital, which moved to campus from San Francisco in 1959. It honors the French chemist and bacteriologist, Louis Pasteur (1822–95).

PEARCE MITCHELL PLACE lies within the Pearce Mitchell condominiums, at Mayfield Avenue and Campus Drive East. The street and the housing complex are named for John Pearce Mitchell (1880–1973), who had a long and influential career at the university and in the Palo Alto community. He received his bachelor's degree at Stanford in 1903, his M.A. in 1904, and (after a year at the University of Leipzig) his Ph.D. in 1909. Joining the Stanford faculty as an acting instructor in 1905, he rose to become professor of chemistry in 1920. His specialty was air and water pollution. For decades, Mitchell was a member of the Board of Athletic Control, a semi-independent body responsible for managing Stanford's intercollegiate athletic program, serving both as its treasurer for the board's 26 years of existence (1917–43) and its secretary (1920–43). He rescued the Associated Students of Stanford University (ASSU) from bankruptcy, and played an important role in redefining the Lower Division program. Mitchell is perhaps best remembered as university registrar (1925–45) and academic secretary. His civic involvement included the Palo Alto city council from 1930 to 1961 and two terms as mayor, from 1951 to 1953. In his honor, the city dedicated J. Pearce Mitchell Park in 1957. (Pearce is properly pronounced *purse*.)

John Pearce Mitchell

PETER COUTTS CIRCLE runs through the Peter Coutts faculty residential subdivision, just off **PETER COUTTS ROAD**. Peter Coutts was a pseudonym for Jean-Baptiste Paulin Caperon, sometimes referred to as "the mysterious Frenchman" (whence the names Frenchman's Road and Frenchman's Hill). A wealthy, well-educated banker, bibliophile, and socialist, Caperon emigrated from France to California in 1874. He acquired the Matadero Ranch in Mayfield in 1875 and established a 1,400-acre stock farm and dairy. In 1881, Caperon returned to France and a year later sold the estate to Leland Stanford for $140,000. The streets and lands that refer to Peter Coutts lie within this property. Caperon died in 1889 (his birth date is unknown).

★ **PINE AVENUE** was once an important road crossing the campus. It is now included in the straight section of Campus Drive East that begins at Palm Drive. It was probably named for the many conifers that populated the arboretum. At one time, Pine Avenue ran west of Palm Drive as far as the Stanford Mausoleum.

PINE HILL ROAD, a street in the Pine Hill I residential area, connects Alvarado Row and Bowdoin Street. While Pine Hill Road is itself neither hilly nor forested

Jean-Baptiste Paulin Caperon

with pines, it does run toward Pine Hill, which is between Frenchman's Road and Stanford Avenue.

★ **PLUM TREE LANE** was the name for what is essentially the portion of today's Roth Way that runs between Lasuen Street and Lomita Drive.

★ **POLO ROAD** ran at a sharp angle off Pine Avenue (now Campus Drive East), through an area devoted to athletics. Polo was played on campus at various times as a minor sport, especially by students enrolled in ROTC.

★ **PORTOLA STREET** was named by David Starr Jordan in honor of the Spanish explorer Gaspar de Portolá, who first sighted (but did not explore) San Francisco Bay (1769) and confirmed the location of Monterey Bay (1770), prompting the establishment of California's second mission and first presidio. At first this street ran only from Lomita to Lasuen, directly behind the Quad. Later it was extended eastward to Stanford Avenue. Today, the original Portola Street is Escondido Mall, which leads to Meyer Library and continues a little beyond that point, eventually becoming Escondido Road, like Pearce Mitchell Place a street with bollards in its midsection.

QUARRY ROAD runs from El Camino Real alongside the Stanford Shopping Center, past Leland Stanford's winery (today's Stanford Barn), to the Medical Center. At one time, the road continued to an old sandstone quarry near the site of the 18th hole of the Stanford Golf Course.

QUILLEN COURT, in Escondido Village, is named for Isaac James Quillen (1909–67), a professor in the School of Education. Quillen received a bachelor's degree from the University of Delaware (1929) and master's from Yale (1932), completing his Yale Ph.D. (1942) while serving on the Stanford faculty, which he had joined in 1936, becoming a full professor in 1946. Quillen was recognized internationally for his leadership in developing social studies programs for the schools. (He helped to establish UNESCO and served in Paris for a year in 1948–49 as a member of its secretariat.) From 1953 to 1966, he was dean of the School of Education, guiding the school from a general service program to one specializing in teaching and research at the graduate level; he also promoted the integration of educational research with theory in the social sciences.

RAIMUNDO WAY runs down from Cedro Way in Pine Hill II, crosses Stanford Avenue and then winds through Frenchman's Hill to Peter Coutts Road, just opposite Peter Coutts Circle. The street name refers to Rancho Cañada de Raymundo, a large Mexican land grant situated in today's San Mateo County, north of Searsville Lake and generally west of Crystal Springs Reservoir. This oak-studded land was purchased in 1842 by Englishman John Copinger, who provided a haven for deserting sailors and whiskey makers. Dennis Martin bought part of it in 1846, and in 1882 Leland Stanford purchased 863 acres of the Martin land from Martin's son-in-law, James Dixon.

Isaac James Quillen

★ **RESERVOIR DRIVE** was a circular street named for the small reservoir atop San Juan Hill. Access to Reservoir Drive was from Andreas Avenue to the west, Santa Ynez Street to the south, and Mirada Avenue to the east. The street is now called Mirada Avenue.

★ **RIVERA** † was named for Captain Don Fernando de Rivera y Moncada, a military officer in the Portolá party. He was later appointed governor of Alta California. Though this street is mentioned in David Starr Jordan's *The Days of a Man*, its precise location is not known.

ROBLE DRIVE runs off Santa Teresa Street toward Roble Hall. The name is derived from the Spanish word for deciduous oak tree, specifically *Quercus lobata*, the valley oak or California white oak (whereas Encina, as in Encina Hall, is the *Quercus agrifolia* or coast live oak). Both species thrive on campus.

ROTH WAY honors Almon Roth (1886–1964), a member of the class of 1909 and president of the Associated Students of Stanford University. In 1912, he earned his law degree at Stanford. He served as controller of the university (1919–37) and on the Board of Trustees (1940–43). Roth played a key role in many improvements to campus lands and buildings, as well as needed

Almon Roth

reform of university construction supervision and improvements to water, fire, and police services. He persuaded the Board of Trustees to provide land and financing for the Stanford Golf Course in 1930. Another of his important projects was Frost Amphitheater. Roth was also noted as a waterfront peacemaker for his contribution to settling disputes between shipping companies and longshoremen in San Francisco. Roth Way, once called Plum Tree Lane, occupies a rather prominent position in the overall design of the university, running perpendicular to Palm Drive and connecting Lomita Drive and Lasuen Street and now serving as a shortcut between Campus Drive and the front of the Quadrangle. An unnamed street in about this location appears in Olmsted's 1888 "Plan of Central Premises."

RUNNING FARM LANE is little more than a stub leading from Escondido Road to a parking lot that serves the Rains housing complex. Insignificant as this street may seem today, it was once much longer, and its name is linked to an interesting historical detail. During Peter Coutts's ownership, the area now bordered by El Camino Real and Escondido Road, from Stanford Avenue roughly to Galvez Street, was a thoroughbred horse farm, complete with a racetrack. After acquiring Coutts's property in 1882, Leland Stanford continued this operation as the Running Farm to distinguish it from the larger Trotting Farm Department located west of the reservoir on his Palo Alto Farm.

RYAN COURT, a relative newcomer among the streets of Stanford, is named for Harris Joseph Ryan (1866–1934), who came to Stanford from Cornell in 1905 to head the Electrical Engineering Department. After years of research in electrical power transmission, in 1926 he established a laboratory for the study of high-voltage electricity in a large corrugated metal barn on the south side of Stanford Avenue (not far from the corner of Raimundo Way). It was funded by major utilities interested in long-distance power transmission. The lab's opening featured a spectacular display of six 2.1-million-volt flashovers through 20 feet of air between electrodes. Ryan later helped solve problems of long-distance power transmission between Hoover Dam and the city of Los Angeles. From 1959 to 1973, the laboratory housed a small nuclear reactor for academic study, and later was used for university storage. The building was demolished in 1988, and 26 faculty/staff townhouses were built on the site. Ryan Court is the approach from Stanford Avenue to this housing cluster.

SALVATIERRA STREET, one of the oldest residential streets, was named by President David Starr Jordan for Juan María Salvatierra (1648–1717), an Italian-born Jesuit priest stationed in New Spain (Mexico). He was the first to urge the founding of missions in Alta California. In 1697, Salvatierra founded Loreto, the first Spanish settlement in Baja California.

SAM McDONALD MALL (initially ROAD when constructed in 1941) is a pedestrian way named for the much-loved Emanuel B. "Sam" McDonald (1884–1957). He

Harris Joseph Ryan   Emanuel B. "Sam" McDonald

was hired in 1903 as a teamster, appointed caretaker of athletic properties in 1907, and later became superintendent of athletic buildings and grounds, the first African American to hold a supervisory position at Stanford. Generations of Stanford students remember him for his generosity and mentoring of undergraduates as well as for his famous barbecues benefiting the Stanford Children's Convalescent Home. Sam McDonald County Park occupies land near La Honda in the Santa Cruz Mountains that McDonald left to the university, which sold it to San Mateo County. He wrote his reminiscences in *Sam McDonald's Farm,* published in 1954. This pedestrian path connects Mel Nelson Mall to Campus Drive East on one side of a large parking lot, and on the other side runs to El Camino Real.

SAMUEL MORRIS WAY is only one block long, connecting Panama and Santa Teresa Streets alongside Terman Engineering Center, headquarters of the School of Engineering. The street is named for Samuel Brooks Morris (1890–1962), a member of the Stanford class of 1911. In 1936, Morris left a successful career as a practicing hydraulic engineer to become Stanford's second dean of engineering, a position he held until 1945. He left academia to become general manager and chief engineer of the Los Angeles Department of Water and

Samuel Brooks Morris

Power. Morris was a noted figure in the field of water resources and dam construction, and was the designer and builder of what came to be called the Morris Dam in San Gabriel Canyon. It was dedicated in 1933 by another Stanford alumnus: Herbert Hoover, class of 1895.

SAND HILL ROAD runs from El Camino Real to Searsville Lake in the foothills. The portion that borders the campus, at one time called Willow Road, is an extension of the original Sand Hill Road. The remainder follows the old Mayfield-Searsville Road, one of the earliest thoroughfares in the area. On early maps, it is variously labeled Searsville Road and Mayfield Road. From the 1850s, a stage followed this route up to the old town of Searsville. The name Sand Hill reflects the old road's condition, which went from knee-deep dust in summer to nearly impassible adobe mud after winter rains.

SAN FRANCISCO COURT and **SAN FRANCISCO TERRACE** are among several streets in the Pine Hill I residential subdivision named for California missions. These two refer to Mission San Francisco de Asís, which was completed in 1791 and is on Dolores Street in San Francisco. This church is better known as Mission Dolores.

SAN JUAN STREET, dating from the university's early days, connects to Santa Ynez. It refers to Mission San Juan Capistrano, in present-day Orange County. President David Starr Jordan, who used names from California's Spanish history for many streets in this neighborhood, had been particularly impressed with this mission. San Juan Street was among the second (circa 1900) batch of streets to be developed as faculty housing. Once crossing Santa Ynez Street and connecting to Dolores Street, it now consists of two disconnected parts, a stub off Santa Ynez and a loop road that curls from Dolores to Cabrillo.

SAN RAFAEL PLACE is a block-long street off Mayfield Avenue in the Pine Hill I faculty residential subdivision. The name refers to Mission San Rafael Arcángel, which was founded as a hospital *asistencia* (sanitarium) for Mission Dolores in 1817 and became a mission in 1823. San Rafael is the patron saint of good health. The mission is in the city of San Rafael in Marin County.

SANTA FE AVENUE is located in Pine Hill I off Mayfield Avenue. In Spanish, Santa Fe means "holy faith."

SANTA MARIA STREET is named for Father Vicente Santa María, an associate of Father Serra and Father Lasuén. The block-long street connects Junipero Serra Boulevard and Gerona Road in the old campus residential subdivision.

SANTA TERESA STREET runs from the back of Tresidder Union to Campus Drive West. It has been suggested that the street was named for Saint Teresa, patron saint of missions. But more likely it was named after Santa Teresa de Avila (1515–82) or perhaps for the Santa Teresa Hills near New Almaden, south of San Jose. The Greystone Quarry there provided the sandstone used in building the Stanford Quadrangle. David Starr Jordan may have named this early campus road, one of three parallel streets directly behind the Quad. SANTA TERESA LANE is in the Searsville Block residential area, just off Governor's Avenue.

SANTA YNEZ STREET is one of the original streets in the old campus residential area. Ynez is a variant of Inés, which is Spanish for Agnes. Mission Santa Inés, founded in 1804 in the Santa Ynez Valley near today's town of

Solvang, is named for her. The extent of Santa Ynez Street has changed over time. Indeed, the portion of Santa Ynez that once linked Reservoir Drive and Cabrillo Street was eliminated and replaced by the portion of Cabrillo Street that ran as far as Andreas Avenue.

SEARSVILLE ROAD and **SEARSVILLE PATH** are remnants of an important early road that led from the town of Mayfield, across the west side of the Quad to a bridge over San Francisquito Creek (near the present-day Oak Creek Apartments and what was then Cedro Cottage). This portion connected to the road (known today as Sand Hill Road) that led up to the timberlands, sawmills, horse racing, and boisterous saloons of the town of Searsville. The town grew up around a mill and forge established at the base of the Old La Honda Road by Dennis Martin in 1851 but took its name from the Sears Hotel, built in 1854 by forty-niner John H. Sears. Searsville Lake was formed near the already vanishing town in 1890. (See MAYFIELD Road.)

SEQUOIA LANE is a service road running from the Packard Electrical Engineering Building to the South Service Road, alongside Stone Pine Plaza of the Science and Engineering Quad. The new Sequoia Hall, home of the Statistics Department, is nearby. The street takes its name from the genus of California's native red-woods given by botanist Stephen Endlicher; it honors Sequoyah, creator of the Cherokee alphabet. SEQUOIA WAY runs between the Hansen Experimental Physics Lab (HEPL) and Green Earth Sciences, ending at Panama Street.

SERRA STREET and **SERRA MALL** were named for Father Junípero Serra (1713–84), the Franciscan missionary and founder of the first nine missions in Alta California.

In 1731, Serra entered the Franciscan Order and adopted the religious name Junípero after a companion of
Saint Francis of Assisi. Governor José de Gálvez selected Father Serra to establish Franciscan missions in Alta
California. The first of these was founded in 1769. He
presided over the system from mission San Carlos
Borromeo de Carmelo (Mission Carmel). University
President David Starr Jordan selected the name Serra
for this very important early campus street, which runs
directly along the front of the Quadrangle. Jordan was
impressed by Serra's passion, energy, and vision. Serra
Mall, between Via Ortega and Galvez Street, is now
closed to general automotive traffic. Serra Street leads
from Galvez Street to El Camino Real near the eastern
corner of the campus.

SONOMA TERRACE, in the Pine Hill I faculty residential
area, is named for the 21st (and last) of the California
missions, in today's city of Sonoma. This church was
founded in 1823 as Mission San Francisco Solano in
honor of a distinguished missionary to Peru but is
known simply as the Sonoma Mission. Among several
theories on the origin of the name Sonoma, one has it
that the word was applied to an Indian tribe in the early
19th century; another that it is derived from a Patwin
(tribe) word for "nose"; and another a connection with
Sonoma County's Valley of the Moon based on an
indigenous term for "many moons" Or did it come from
a Mayakmah (tribe) word *noma,* meaning "town"?

SOUTH SERVICE ROAD links a parking area across
Via Ortega from parking structure 2 to the back of the
McCullough Building.

STANFORD AVENUE extends from Junipero Serra
Boulevard (JSB) across El Camino Real to Park Avenue

in Palo Alto. Stanford Avenue between JSB and Amherst Street (in Palo Alto) is a county road. It is newer than the remainder, which is a Palo Alto city street bordering the Palo Alto neighborhood known as College Terrace and Stanford's Escondido Village. The streets of College Terrace bear the names of colleges and universities, though this was not always the case: Cornell Street was called Washington Street, and California Avenue was called Lincoln Avenue. The portion of Stanford Avenue between Amherst Street and El Camino Real was once called Mayfield Avenue. (See MAYFIELD AVENUE and RUNNING FARM LANE.)

STOCK FARM ROAD, opened in 1985, connects Sand Hill Road and Oak Road to Campus Drive West. It roughly marks the north end of the Trotting Farm Department of the Palo Alto Stock Farm and its mile-long oval track, which were located in this area to the west of the original Governor's Avenue. The heart of Leland Stanford's "farm," the trotting horse barns, paddocks, tracks, shops, and employee buildings housed some 600 horses and 150 men at its peak in the early 1890s. It was one of the most successful trotting horse establishments of its day (1878–1903), garnering 19 world records. The Red Barn equestrian area was substantially restored in 1984.

Leland Stanford Jr.

SWAIN WAY, in the Stanford West Apartments subdivision, honors Robert Eckles Swain (1875–1961), professor of chemistry and a key figure in the administration of university president Ray Lyman Wilbur. Swain, Stanford class of 1899, studied biochemistry at Yale University and received a master's degree in 1901 and a Ph.D. in 1904 after study in Europe. He joined the Stanford faculty in 1898, and was chairman of the Chemistry Department from 1917 to 1940. Between 1929 and 1933, he served as vice president and acting president of the university while President Wilbur was Herbert Hoover's secretary of the interior. Swain did pioneering work in atmospheric pollution, especially related to smelter smoke. A member of the Palo Alto City Council from 1912 to 1921, Swain also served three times as mayor of Palo Alto.

THOBURN COURT in Escondido Village, just off Serra Street, is named for Wilbur Wilson Thoburn (1859–99), professor of bionomics. A Methodist minister, he served as Stanford's unofficial chaplain and counselor to many students from 1893 until his death, in 1899. He was the first—and only—faculty member buried at the short-lived cemetery near the Stanford Family Mausoleum. He is also listed among the city fathers of Palo Alto. In 1902, a school for girls was opened in Palo Alto

Robert Eckles Swain

Wilbur Wilson Thoburn

and named after him, although it was subsequently renamed Miss Harker's School.

TOLMAN DRIVE and its appendages **NORTH TOLMAN DRIVE** and **SOUTH TOLMAN DRIVE** lie within the Frenchman's Hill residential subdivision. They are named for Cyrus Fisher Tolman (1873–1942), a professor of economic geology—the understanding of ore deposits, petroleum, and ground water—in the Department of Geology. Tolman was a national collegiate doubles champion in tennis at the University of Chicago, from which he graduated in 1896. He served with the U.S. Army in Cuba during the Spanish-American War. Tolman, nicknamed "Chief," came to Stanford in 1912 and taught until he retired in 1938.

VALDEZ PLACE in Pine Hill II residential subdivision is named for Juan Bautista Valdéz, a member of the Juan Bautista de Anza party. De Anza's two expeditions (1774, 1776) established a practical overland trail from Sonora to California through Arizona, and thereby enabled the system of missions in Alta California to flourish. It was Valdéz who carried the order from the viceroy to Juan Bautista de Anza to start the expedition from Sonora to San Gabriel.

Cyrus Fisher Tolman

VALPARAISO STREET is one of the original streets in the first residential area on campus. It was presumably named for the important 19th-century Pacific trading post and seaport in Chile through which many Gold Rush hopefuls passed en route to California. Interestingly, Valparaiso, Chile, is called Pancho, a nickname for Francisco, which is a reference to the city's association with its trading partner, San Francisco.

VARIAN WAY lies within the Stanford West Apartments subdivision. This street honors brothers Russell (1898–1959) and Sigurd (1901–61) Varian, co-inventors, with physics Professor William W. Hansen, of the rhumbatron and klystron tubes, precursors to microwave technology. From their youth, it became clear that Russell had a talent for invention and Sigurd had a knack for building his brother's inventions. An expert electrician, Sigurd was also a keen aviator. (Thus, the title of the book written by Russell's widow, Dorothy: *The Inventor and the Pilot*.) Russell earned his bachelor's degree in 1925 and his master's in 1927 in physics, both at Stanford. Sigurd enrolled at California Polytechnic School in San Luis Obispo, but after a semester and a half, he grew restless with studies and left to find a job. Sigurd began taking flying lessons in 1922, and two years later bought an O.X.5 Jenny,

Russell Varian   Sigurd Varian

a World War I plane. Later he became a pilot for Pan American Airlines. The brothers are best known for the company, Varian Associates, which they founded in 1948 in collaboration with Stanford professor Edward Ginzton and others. This was some 11 years after they had collaborated with Professor Hansen on the klystron tube, a device having a velocity-modulated electron stream that may be used for the amplification of microwaves or as an oscillator. During World War II, the klystron became an integral component of radar.

VERNIER PLACE, in the Frenchman's Hill residential sub-division, is named for Chester G. Vernier (1881–1949), professor of law from 1916 until his retirement in 1946. He received his B.A. degree from Butler University (1904), and B. Phil. (1904) and J.D. (1907) from the University of Chicago. He taught law at Indiana University, and the universities of Nebraska and Illinois before joining the Stanford faculty. A prolific writer and exacting teacher, Vernier is noted for his six-volume treatise *American Family Laws.* His other specialties included criminal law, criminology, and commercial law.

★ **VIA CRESPI** was named by David Starr Jordan to honor Father Juan Crespí (1721–82), a Franciscan who studied philosophy under Junípero Serra. Years later,

Chester G. Vernier

he served as chaplain and diarist with Portolá's first expedition to locate Monterey Bay (1769–70) and accompanied the second successful Monterey search party (1770). He is buried next to Junípero Serra at Carmel Mission. Little is left of this street, which until the 1990s ran northward from Panama Street to Via Pueblo, behind the Durand, McCullough, and Varian buildings.

VIA ORTEGA, between Panama Street and Campus Drive West, is presumably named for José Ortega, a scout with the Portolá expedition. It is said that Sergeant Ortega's scouting party discovered and named San Francisco Bay on November 2, 1769, viewing it from what is now called Sweeney Ridge near the town of Pacifica in San Mateo County.

VIA PALOU, part service road and part mall, is named after missionary Francisco Palóu (1723–89), a Franciscan who accompanied Father Junípero Serra to the missions of New Spain (Mexico) in 1749. For nearly 25 years, Palóu held a succession of important ecclesiastical positions in Mexico and Baja California. Later, he took charge of the Alta California missions in the absence of Junipero Serra. There he was reunited with his boyhood friend, Father Juan Crespí. In 1774 and 1775, Palóu was a diarist on two expeditions to San Francisco. He founded Mission San Francisco de Asís in 1776, and served there until 1785. In 1784, he presided over the burial of Junípero Serra and took over his duties as acting president of the missions. Palóu is also noted for his book on the life of Junipero Serra, which is said to be the first book ever written in California.

VIA PUEBLO, in the west campus area, is a service road alongside the Allen Center for Integrated Systems, the

Packard Electrical Engineering Building, and Sequoia Hall, connecting Via Ortega and Lomita Mall. *Pueblo* means "village" in Spanish. In California, the pueblo— or settlement for colonists—had its own regular governing body. The first of these, the pueblo of San José de Guadalupe (today's city of San Jose) was founded in 1777. Pueblo was also the name given to the settled agricultural areas developed to support and sustain life in the mission system. There was a pueblo at Sonoma (see SONOMA TERRACE).

VINEYARD LANE runs from Quarry Road through the Stanford Shopping Center to Sand Hill Road, passing through an area that was once an extensive vineyard near the Stanford residence. Leland Stanford, an ardent believer in California's wine industry, had three vineyards: the Palo Alto vineyard and winery (originally housed in the red brick building now restored as the Stanford Barn), a large vineyard at Warm Springs, near Mission San Jose (in Fremont), and at Vina, in Tehama County. There, Stanford built a state-of-the-art winemaking and storage facility, imported French vineyard workers, and planted more than two dozen varieties of grapes. By the mid-1880s, with nearly 4,000 acres planted, Vina was the largest vineyard in the world. That it never produced the quality of wine expected is more likely because of soil and climate conditions rather than to the owner's level of investment.

VISTA LANE lies in the foothills across Junipero Serra Boulevard, off Links Road. The name is derived from *Alta Vista,* home of Charles Lathrop, university treasurer and Mrs. Stanford's youngest brother. Just off Links Road, this short street leads, fittingly, to an observatory. (See ALTA ROAD.)

WELCH ROAD forms half the perimeter of the Medical Center from Quarry Road to Campus Drive West. It honors a major medical figure, William Henry Welch (1850–1934), sometimes called the dean of American Medicine. Dr. Welch was the first dean of the School of Medicine at Johns Hopkins University.

WING PLACE is a cul-de-sac in the Frenchman's Hill residential subdivision. It is named for Charles Benjamin Wing (1864–1945), professor of structural engineering at Stanford from 1892 to 1945 (emeritus 1929) and head of the Civil Engineering Department from 1923 to 1929. Wing received his engineering degree from Cornell in 1886, and served as instructor in civil engineering at Cornell and professor of bridge and hydraulic engineering at Wisconsin before coming to Stanford at the request of President David Starr Jordan. An authority on highway construction, he also consulted on construction of Hetch Hetchy Dam and construction of bridges in Oregon and Washington. Following the 1906 earthquake, which killed two at Stanford and severely damaged university buildings and other structures, Wing was one of three engineering professors (the others being William F. Durand and Charles Marx) who were appointed to assess damage and oversee reconstruction. These three colleagues

Charles Benjamin Wing

also designed and supervised construction of Stanford's football stadium, which was inaugurated at the Stanford–Cal Big Game of November 19, 1921. He donated his fee to establish a scholarship fund for civil engineering students. An active civic leader, Wing served as mayor of Palo Alto in 1910 and 1911, and was a member of the city council for 20 years. He also played a key role in the movement to preserve California's redwood forests, and as chief of the Division of Parks was instrumental in increasing the number of state parks from 3 to 80.

SOURCES

MAPS

Stanford University maps from the turn of the century to the 1950s are included in the yearly *Stanford University Annual Register* (a combined university directory and course catalog). Historic maps of the campus are available in the Maps and Records office, the Stanford University Archives, and the Branner Geology Library. Of special note are:

Hoss, Della Taylor. *Stanford University Campus* (Stanford University Press, 1950). Stanford University Archives, Map 405.

King, P.S. *The Campus of Stanford University at Palo Alto, California* (Stanford University Press, ca.1956). Stanford University Archives, Map 300.

Map of Campus, Leland Stanford Junior University, Palo Alto, Santa Clara County, Calif...compiled for Insurance Purposes, October 1917. Stanford University Archives, Map 801.

Map of the Lands of the Leland Stanford Junior University...Surveyed for the Board of Trustees of the University by A.T. and F.A. Herrmann, 1908. Stanford University Archives, Map 700.

Map of the Leland Stanford Jr. University and Surroundings at Palo Alto, Cal. 1891. Compiled by C.H. Herker. Stanford University Archives, Map 200.

Sanborn Fire Insurance maps, California, 1895-1949 [microfilm]. Original maps published by Sanborn Map Company.

Taylor, Della. *Map Showing Stanford University, Present and Future.* (Stanford University Press, 1928). Stanford University Archives, Map 400a.

PUBLICATIONS

Adamson, Maud. *The Land Grant System of Governor Juan B. Alvarado.* Unpublished masters thesis, Department of History, University of Southern California, 1931.

Allen, Peter C. "The Cottage by the Creek." *Sandstone & Tile* (Stanford Historical Society) 9, no. 3 (Spring 1985): 2-9.

Allen, Peter C. *Stanford: From the Foothills to the Bay.* Stanford, Calif.: Stanford Alumni Association/Stanford Historical Society, 1980.

Arbuckle, Clyde. *Santa Clara County Ranchos.* 2d ed. San Jose, Calif.: Rosicrucian Press, 1973.

Bartholomew, Karen. *Stanford's Red Barn.* Stanford, Calif.: Stanford Historical Society, 1984.

Bartholomew, Karen. "The Design of a University." *Stanford Observer* (Stanford News Service, April 1987), special section.

Bartholomew, Karen, Claude Brinegar, and Roxanne Nilan. *A Chronology of Stanford University and its Founders, 1824-2000.* Stanford, Calif.: Stanford Historical Society, 2001.

Bean, Walton, and James Rawls. *California: An Interpretive History.* 5th ed. New York: McGraw-Hill, 1988.

Bolton, Herbert Eugene. *Fray Juan Crespi, Missionary Explorer On The Pacific Coast, 1769-1774.* Berkeley, Calif.: University of California Press, 1927.

Butler, Phyllis Filiberti. *Old Santa Clara Valley.* San Carlos, Calif.: Wide World Publishing/Tetra, 1991.

Cain, Julie, and Roxanne Nilan. "Stanford's Arboretum, 1885-1905." *Sandstone & Tile* 25, no. 1 (summer 2003): 3-10.

Clark, Birge M. *Memoir About Mr. and Mrs. Herbert Hoover, with Particular Emphasis on the Planning and Building of Their Home on San Juan Hill.* Palo Alto, Calif.: privately printed, 1969.

Clausen, Henry C. *Stanford's Judge Crothers: The Life Story of George E. Crothers.* San Francisco: The George E. Crothers Trust, 1967.

Crothers, George E. *Founding of the Leland Stanford Junior University.* San Francisco: A.M. Robertson, 1932 (rep. from *Americana* (American Historical Society) 26, no. 2 (April 1932).

Davis, Margo, and Roxanne Nilan. *The Stanford Album: A Photographic History, 1885-1945.* Stanford, Calif.: Stanford University Press, 1989.

Duffus, R.L. *The Innocents at Cedro: A Memoir of Thorstein Veblen and Some Others.* New York: Macmillan, 1944.

Elliott, Ellen Coit. *It Happened This Way: American Scene.* Stanford, Calif.: Stanford University Press, 1940.

Elliott, Orrin Leslie. *Stanford University: the First Twenty-Five Years.* Stanford, Calif.: Stanford University Press, 1937.

Elliott, Orrin Leslie, and O. V. Eaton. *Stanford University and Thereabouts*. San Francisco: Murdock Printers, 1896.

Fifty Years on the Quad: A Pictorial Record of Stanford University and the 35,000 Men and Women Who Have Spent a Part of Their Lives on the Campus 1887-1937. Norris E. James, ed. Stanford, Calif.: Stanford Alumni Association, 1938.

Flexner, Simon, and Thomas Flexner. *William Henry Welch and the Heroic Age of American Medicine*. New York: Viking Press, 1941.

Ginzton, Edward L. "The $100 Idea." *IEEE Spectrum* 12, no. 2 (February 1975): 30-39.

Griego, Elizabeth. *A Part and Yet Apart: Clelia Duel Mosher and Professional Women at the Turn-of-the-Century*. Unpublished Ph.D. dissertation, University of California, Berkeley, 1983.

Gudde, Edwin G. *California Place Names*. 4th ed. Berkeley, Calif.: University of California Press, 1998.

Guest, Francis F. *Fermin Francisco de Lasuen*. Washington, D.C.: Academy of American Franciscan History, 1973.

Gullard, Pamela and Nancy Lund. *History of Palo Alto*. San Francisco: Scottwall Associates, 1989.

Harlow, Neal. *California Conquered: War and Peace on the Pacific, 1846-1850*. Berkeley, Calif.: University of California Press, 1982.

Historic Houses of San Juan Hill. Stanford, Calif.: Stanford Historical Society, 1995.

Historic Houses of Lower San Juan District. Stanford, Calif.: Stanford Historical Society, 1998.

Historical Atlas Map of Santa Clara County. California. San Francisco, Calif.: Thompson and West Publishing Company, 1876.

Holmes, Norman W. *Prune Country Railroading.* Huntington Beach, Calif.: Shade Tree Books, 1995.

Hoover, Mildred Brooke, et al. *Historic Spots in California.* (5th ed., rev. by Douglas E. Kyle). Stanford, Calif.: Stanford University Press, 2002.

Johnson, Paul C., et al., eds. *The California Missions.* Menlo Park, Calif.: Lane Book Company, 1974.

Joncas, Richard, David J. Neuman and Paul V. Turner. *The Campus Guide: Stanford University.* New York: Princeton Architectural Press, 1999.

Jordan, David Starr. *The Days of a Man: Being Memories of a Naturalist, Teacher and Minor Prophet of Democracy.* Yonkers-on-Hudson, N.Y.: World Book Co., 1922.

Kimball, Margaret, et al. "Miracle on Palm Drive," *Sandstone & Tile* 18, no. 4 (fall 1994): 1-16.

Kirkwood, Marion R., and William B. Owens. *A Brief History of the Stanford Law School, 1893-1946.* Stanford, Calif.: School of Law, Stanford University, 1961.

Littleboy, Jeff. "The Sam McDonald Story." *Sandstone & Tile* 7: no. 2 (winter 1983): 1-10.

Long, Linda. "Professor Earl Barnes Love Affair Cost Him His Stanford Position." *Stanford Historical Society Quarterly* 6, no. 3 (spring-summer 1982): 6.

MacDougall, Laurie. *Henry Cowell and His Family.* San Francisco: S.H. Cowell Foundation, 1989.

Mahood, James, and **Kristine Wenburg, eds.,** *The Mosher Study: Sexual Attitudes of 45 Women.* New York: Arno Press, 1980.

Marinacci, Barbara, and **Rudy Marinacci.** *California's Spanish Place Names.* 2d ed. Houston, Tx: Gulf Publishing Company, 1997.

Marschner, Janice. *California 1850: A Snapshot in Time.* Sacramento: Coleman Ranch Press, 2002.

"Mayfield, 1850-1925." *The Tall Tree* (Palo Alto Historical Association) 4, no. 1 (May 1976).

McCaleb, Charles S. *Tracks, Tires and Wires.* Glendale, Calif: Interurban Press, 1981.

McDonald, Emanuel B. *Sam McDonald's Farm.* Stanford, Calif.: Stanford University Press, 1954.

Mears, Gladys Chute. *Elliott Grinnell Mears.* Stanford, Calif.: Privately printed for the author by Stanford University Press, 1947.

Mitchell, J. Pearce. *Stanford University, 1916-1941.* Stanford, Calif.: Stanford University Press, 1958.

Moffat, Shannon. "Stanford's Power Line Research Pioneers." *Sandstone and Tile* 12, no. 1 (fall 1987): 3-7.

"Nathan Abbott." *Columbia Law Review* 41: 4 (April 1941):
577-584.

Nilan, Roxanne. "The Life and Times of a Victorian Woman:
Jane Lathrop Stanford." *Sandstone and Tile* 21, no. 3 (summer
1997): 3-14.

Osborne, Carol M. *Museum Builders in the West: The
Stanfords as Collectors and Patrons of Art, 1870-1906.*
Stanford, Calif.: Stanford University Museum of Art, 1986.

Palou, Francisco. *Founding of the First California Missions.*
San Francisco: Nueva California Press, 1934.

Palou, Francisco. *Historical Memoirs of the New California.*
Berkeley, Calif.: University of California Press, 1976.

"Parks of Palo Alto," *The Tall Tree* (Palo Alto Historical
Association) 5, no. 1 (October 1983).

Pourade, Richard F. *Anza Conquers the Desert.* San Diego:
Union-Tribune Publishing Co., 1971.

Regnery, Dorothy. *An Enduring Heritage: An Architectural
History of the San Francisco Peninsula.* Stanford, Calif.:
Stanford University Press, 1976.

Regnery, Dorothy. "Coutts Was No Eccentric." *Stanford
Historical Society Newsletter* 5, no. 3 (summer 1981): 3-6.

Regnery, Dorothy. "Dennis Martin Once Owned Stanford's
Backlands." *Stanford Historical Society Newsletter* 7, no. 3
(spring 1983): 1-3.

Regnery, Dorothy. *The History of Jasper Ridge: From Searsville Pioneers to Stanford Scientists*. Stanford Calif.: Stanford Historical Society, 1991.

Regnery, Dorothy. "The Stanfords and the Serra Statue at the Presidio Monterey." *Sandstone & Tile* 13, no. 2 (winter 1989): 2-5.

Richards, Gilbert. *Crossroads*. Woodside, Calif.: G. Richards Publications, 1973.

Rolle, Andrew F. *California: A History*. Arlington Heights, Ill.: AHM Publishing Corporation, 1978.

Santa Maria, Vicente. *The First Spanish Entry into San Francisco Bay, 1775*. San Francisco: John Howell, 1971.

Short, William R. *Geology of the Santa Teresa Hills*. Unpublished master's thesis, California State University, Hayward, 1986.

Signor, John. *Southern Pacific's Coast Line*. Wilton, Calif.: Signature Press, 1995.

Stanford Alumni Association. *Stanford Alumnus* (1899-1917); *Stanford Illustrated Review* (1917-1940); and *Stanford Alumni Review* (1940-1951).

Stanford Alumni Association. *Alumni Directory* (brief faculty biographies included in those issued in 1910, 1931, and 1955).

Stanford University Academic Council. *Memorial Resolutions*.

Stanford University. *Report of the President*, 1903-1948.

"The Streets of Palo Alto." *The Tall Tree* (Palo Alto Historical Association) 4, no. 2 (rev. ed. 2001).

Terman, Frederick E. "William Frederick Durand." *Biographical Memoirs, National Academy of Sciences* 48 (1976): 153-193.

Turner, Paul V., Marcia E. Vetrocq and Karen Weitze. *The Founders and the Architects: the Design of Stanford University*. Stanford, Calif.: Department of Art, Stanford University, 1976.

Tutorow, Norman E. *Leland Stanford, Man of Many Careers*. Menlo Park, Calif.: Pacific Coast Publishers, 1971.

Tutorow, Norman E. *The Governor: The Life and Legacy of Leland Stanford, A California Colossus*. Spokane, Wash.: Arthur H. Clark Co., 2004.

Varian, Dorothy. *The Inventor and the Pilot*. Palo Alto, Calif.: Pacific Books Publishers, 1983.

Wilbur, Ray Lyman. *The Memoirs of Ray Lyman Wilbur, 1875-1949*. Stanford, Calif.: Stanford University Press, 1960.

Wilson, John L. *Stanford University School of Medicine and the Predecessor Schools: An Historical Perspective*. Stanford, Calif.: Stanford Medical School, Lane Medical Library, 1999. Electronically published as http://eLane.stanford.edu/wilson/home.html.

Winslow, Ward. *Palo Alto: A Centennial History*. Palo Alto, Calif.: Palo Alto Historical Association, 1993.

Wyatt, Roscoe D., and Clyde Arbuckle. *Historic Names, Persons and Places in Santa Clara County.* San Jose, Calif.: Santa Clara County Board of Education, 1948.

Historic photographs courtesy of Stanford University Archives. Cover color photograph courtesy of Stanford News Service.

Inside Back Cover: Central campus portion from *Map of Lands of the Leland Stanford Junior University*, surveyed for the university's Board of Trustees by A.T. and F.A. Herrmann and printed in 1908. (An original full-size printed version can be seen on the wall at the entrance to the Stanford Planning Office.) In 1908, today's Palm Drive was still called University Avenue and was off-limits to cars (which used Automobile Road in the arboretum). The Stock Farm was still much in evidence, not only its former racetracks and paddocks, but also its vineyard and roads, especially Governor's Avenue and Pine Avenue (a portion of today's Campus Drive West).